Presented by
Kay and Bob Dinwiddie
in memory of
Mary Margaret Dolaz
May 1985

Measuring My Days

Measuring My Days

Maureen Fell Pierson

BAKER BOOK HOUSE
Grand Rapids, Michigan

Preface

In the summer of 1971 my wife learned that she had cancer. She insisted upon complete honesty from her doctors, followed their instructions faithfully, accepted the fact that her days were measured, and went on with the business of living with enthusiasm and joy. Often unable to sleep because of pain she expressed her thoughts and feelings in writing.

These short poems were intended only for her family, but they express the cycle of human emotions: loneliness, anger, courage, acceptance, trust, and love. Through them all there is faith in the ultimate goodness of life, and thanksgiving for ordinary things and for the mystery and wonder of each day.

During forty years in the ministry, I have noticed that the people who love life the most have the least fear of death. Believing life to be good they know that the Giver of life must be good, and, since death is part of His plan, it cannot be evil.

I hope that the faith these poems reflect will inspire others, and help them to celebrate life and live it to the fullest until death: "that moment when dying ends."

Clifford J. Pierson

Measuring My Days

A Hand reined me in.
Held back, I struggled,
strained to go as I had gone:
hard,
fast.

The Hand held firm.
I found it quieting me,
gentling me,
coaxing me into another pace.

I would have missed so much
if all my life had been a race.

Hold my hand.
Hold me in your arms.
The holding holds so much.
Hold my hand.
Hold me in your arms.
Hold me.

Why is it so important
to be touched?
Is it because
this sensuous body
longs to remain corporeal,
needs reassurance,
protests becoming dust?

There are times
when I feel like crying.

I looked at myself
in the mirror tonight.
I am alive.
Someday I won't be.

There are times.

I do not dry
the tears
that flow
from eyes
to cheek
to pillow.

I exist.
My tears exist.
If they don't fall
tonight,
can laughter rise
tomorrow?

The priest and priestess
of radiology
leave,
having conducted their ritual.

The guardian door
sighs shut.
I lie upon
a high steel altar
in chapel dimness—
golden polygon lit.

A great footfall,
an expansive breath.
The finger of God
enters my bone.

You're kind,
young doctor,
to verbalize
what you think
are my fears.
In a deft juggling,
you toss them
before me skillfully,
so they do not
obscure the hope
you also throw out.
Thank you.
Your kindness
means more
than your words.

The way to the sunrise
lies that way:
upward.

At times
the path is narrow,
rough,
steep.

At times
it opens up,
widens out,
as a gentle slope
reaches a new level.

This side of the summit
there's a tunnel
to pass through
before stepping out
into the dawn light.

I will travel
light
as I journey
toward the sunrise.

Who needs envy,
self-pity,
fear?

They're too heavy for me.

Without them
I feel buoyant,
light.

Have joy,
Will travel.

When illusions
have been torn
to shreds,
and reality
stands
cold, naked, undisguised
before me,
I can no longer
deny nor reject
It.

I must recognize
It
at last.

The kiss of death
has awakened me
to life.
I did not see,
nor hear,
nor feel,
as I do now.

Death's touch,
like a lover's caress,
has left me
shaken
with the beauty
of life.

The memory
of giving birth
comforts me.
I recall
the sustaining power
that came
when I needed it.

And the payoff—
joy!

Isn't life
like an airport?

Human beings
arriving, departing,
good-bye-ing, greeting,
separating, uniting,
parting, meeting.

But, when I take off someday
and disappear from sight,
don't forget
how much I loved the flight.

No one can go with me—
not even you.
Through the years
I've become so used
to your saying,
"I'll take you,"
"I'll go with you."

But when this going comes,
I must depart alone.

Today I want to smile.
I want to be cheerful.
I want to be loving.
But except for a great ache,
I am empty inside.

Today
my eyes are heavy
beneath their lower lashes.
They hold unshed tears.

I feel deep grief
for all the mistakes
I have made
as wife and mother.

Today
I am a jug
filled
with the yeasty wine
of life.
I bubble.
I effervesce.
Joy rises
and works in me.

What can I do
on the dizzy days,
the weak days,
the heartbeat-conscious days,
the shallow breathing days?
I can love.
I can love.

It's hard for a human being
to believe God suffers.
If you or I were He,
we'd arrange things
so we didn't.

But if the incarnation
means anything,
it means that:
God feels.
God suffers.

Don't let the anguish show.
You know
it comes
and goes.
It has come.
It will go.
Don't let it show.

I wake
in the night
and listen
for a sound
of your living,
as on long ago nights
I hung over the crib
of each infant child of ours,
and listened.
I did not turn away
until I was reassured
by the sound of breathing.

Death, come when you must.
I will not run nor hide
as one would from rapist or thief.
I will not frantically flee from you
because I do not think of you
as a criminal who comes to harm or rob.

But to be honest, I do not think
I will ever be ready to welcome you.
Though the time will come, perhaps,
when I shall be able to receive you graciously,
as I have a too-early guest.

I am not afraid of you.
I do not hate the thought of you,
but I like living very much.
So I do not invite you to visit me.
I simply say,
Come when you must.

Alone in the kitchen,
I find I am crying.
I am skating
on thin ice
and it is cracking.
I want to reach out
to keep from going under.
People need people.
But, as Sartre says,
Being
is an individual venture.

I knew
if I had to
I could call you.
And that
was something
to hang on to.

I believe
that doors open
eternally.

Even though
door after door
closes behind
and before me,
never
to open again,
and I must wait
in a dark corridor
not knowing
where nor when
other doors
will open wide.

Some will.
Some always have.
I believe
some always will.

Thank God for paper and pen!
A thought,
a feeling,
can emerge,
take form,
be known
for what it is.

Then,
like an animal
released from a cage,
it is no longer so frantic
that it can't be handled.
Thank God for paper and pen!

In all I see and feel
there is a paradox.
I am limited—
and free.
I feel anguish—
and joy.
I know certainty
within uncertainty.
I contain death and life.

At the heart of life's paradox
is Mystery.
I choose to trust this Mystery.
I ride a bicycle of faith
through patches of shadow
and sunlight,
among living green
and dying red and yellow leaves.

I am enjoying Now.
I have let go of past anger and past grief,
have let them drop down the chasm of time.
I will not live over and over again in memory
events which I experienced only once.

I am not immune to anger and grief.
When they arise out of new events,
I will receive them,
and then let them, too,
fall away from me into the cleft of time.
I will do nothing to retrieve them.

I will not worry about future illness.
I shall die, perhaps painfully,
but I will not imagine over and over again
an event which I shall experience only once.

Life is good, rich, full.
I am enjoying Now.

I thought I learned long ago
that you have to let people love
in their own way.
True expressions of love
are not trained dogs
that jump through a hoop
at a master's bidding.
They are more like
irrepressible puppies
that come running to you
unexpectedly,
if you don't try to catch them.

I've tried to make your love
jump through the hoop
of my conditions.
Long ago I learned that unless
an expression of love
is freely given,
it's not a gift,
but a tax.
It seems I have to learn this
all over again.
Who wants to be a tax collector?

You made me so happy
so unexpectedly, my son.
You came into the kitchen,
kissed me on the cheek,
and said, "I love you."
Each time I recall this
you wouldn't believe
how happy I feel.

I wake from my nap
in the back seat
and open my eyes
to see sky and trees
and mountains
going past
at a crazy angle.
I feel
the companionship
between the two of you,
and I lie quiet and happy,
loving you both very much.

My birthday has come again,
and I feel younger than I did
when it came last year.

Maybe I'll feel
even younger next year
and still younger
the year after that.

But that would be enough!

I'd want to stop
the younging process
lest I go back
to second childhood
or helpless infancy.

I'll settle for less
than three score years,
if I can die
feeling young.

I sense a change in you—
a change that comes, I think,
only through confrontation
with one's own mortality.
We live on borrowed time.
And now
you've joined the ranks
of those who know we do.

Last night
with your head in my lap
we watched
the launching of Apollo 17.
The screen said,
"Farewell to the moon."
We turned to each other.
The light in your eyes
was a young light:
a hello to the moon,
and sky rockets,
and stars.

Wordlessly content,
we lie together,
and that nonsensical saying,
"I'm so happy I could die,"
makes sense.

I happily remember the times
you put your arms around me,
as though the crutches weren't there,
and kissed me in greeting.
It's your way of saying,
"I like you,
I'm glad you're alive."
It made me happy
to greet you today.

My heart contains a place
inhabited by you.

I do not know
how many
hours,
days,
years
remain
for us together.

If I knew
this was
the last day
we'd have together,
how would
I live,
my love,
for you this hour?
What wouldn't matter?
What would?

No, God!
No!
Not yet!
Don't let
our life
together
be over.
Not yet!
Not yet!
Nct yet . . .

Cool wind,
light and fresh,
blowing on my face
through the open window
of my bedroom,
you bring knowledge
that a gift has arrived:
a new day
in which to love
and be joyful.

The weather
inside me
is sunny.

Only once
or twice
has a cloud
of wistfulness
floated across
my sky.

But it did not
obscure the sun.

I can live with uncertainty,
because life is worth celebrating
in spite of its paradox and ambiguity.
So I intend to celebrate life
even through the moment of death,
"the moment when dying ends."

I lost my identity this year,
and I've been searching for it
ever since.
My self-images dissolved,
leaving me naked
and vulnerable,
struggling for physical,
mental, emotional health.

Illness made the ways
I've perceived myself
ill-fitting,
and I have not
surely known
who I am.
Wife, mother,
writer, teacher—
none of these
identify me
as once they did.

But strangely,
through losing myself,
I'm learning who I may be:
a loving human being.
It's what I always
should have been.

I think of myself
as an astronaut
scheduled
for a launching
into the unknown.
The exact date
has not been set;
I am not yet
on the launching pad.
And when I am,
there may be delays
in the countdown.
But the final second
will come.
The launching will
take place.
And my life
will blast off
into the wide blue yonder,
where "light and dark
are both alike to Thee."

There is only
one way to live:
Accept the pain
as an element of life,
a part of its
basic unity.

The giving of pain
cannot be prevented,
but the careless
giving of it
can.

At least,
my bad luck
has come
in good luck form.
I could walk unaided
before I lost
the use of my arm,
my left arm.
Luckily,
the right arm is left!

It was not
your words
but your sorrow
and disappointment
that spoke to me
as we spoke
of Betsy's illness.
And so,
I know
there's not going to be
a miraculous reprieve.
My emotion
runs ahead
Of time and death.
I grieve.

I pray
for a miracle
for you.

A miracle is
anything,
anything at all,
in which you feel
the power of God.

Feel His power
in the therapy.
Feel His power
in the doctor's skill.
Don't be angry with God—
put out your hand to Him.

I'll miss you, friend,
as will so many others.
You had a talent
for friendship.
You enjoyed so much
all the good things of life.

I see that the only way
you could truthfully acknowledge
the goodness of God's gift of life
was to be angry with Him
for taking it from you.

What no one wanted
has happened.

But, like many
an unwanted event,
it contains
a saving possibility.

The too-dependent ones
must now let go of you.

Do they ask themselves
the question
I ask myself,
What did I do
that helped
to bring this on?

Cancer—
the word
connotes,
denotes,
death.

Cancerous ones
are moved
outside the common camp.
I thought
they belonged there, too,
until it happened to me.

So,
why does it hurt so much
to see they think
I am going to be
too busy dying
to really live,
to really matter?

I feel the cancer
has proliferated,
madly multiplied.
Cells of outraged grief
I believed
were destroyed
decades ago.

It was only
a long remission.

I feel sad
after being with you.
You always said,
Don't do anything
you can't tell
your mother.

But you live alone,
and you would brood,
remembering
the terminal illness
of your sister
years ago.
I remember her, too—
how she died,
lingeringly, painfully.
But mostly I remember
how she lived.
Every child should have
an aunt like her.
When I was young,
she and her husband seemed
a royal pair.
My golden trust in her
never tarnished.

You always said,
Don't do anything
you can't tell your mother.
And the little girl in me
wants to tell you I've got cancer.
But the woman
can't.

I wish
before I die—

I could
know the charms
of the girl
our son
will wed,
take
in my arms
a child
of a child
of ours,
and cradle
in my hand
its small head.

My sisters,
"big" sister,
"little" sister,
you are so dear
to me.

You want
to give your blood
to bring
healing to mine.

The doctor says
such a desire
is both
practical and symbolical.

Though
practically,
your desire can do
nothing for me.
symbolically,
it says and does
so much.

O Jesus,
hot tears
wash my face.
Sobs
shake me.
And I do not
even know
why I cry.

I think
it is because
I am no more
than I am:
petty me—
not what I want
to be.

Jesu, Jesu,
deliver me!

After a storm,
when the sky
is bright and clear,
it doesn't seem possible
that it will ever
cloud over again.

I went to your
hospital room, Mary,
and you were gone.
Really gone.

I left,
feeling in my heart
the emptiness of your bed,
remembering
I had held your hand,
and you had said,
"You're a comfort to me."

"You've made my day!"
I said
in response
to your compliment.
Then we walked
down the hall together,
talking, laughing,
and I had the x-ray
that confirmed
what we had both
silently suspected
minutes before.

Always
I will remember
the pleasure that
your spontaneous thoughtfulness,
your well-timed compliment,
gave me.
That pleasure sat with me
as I waited for the x-ray,
knowing in my bones
I was to receive
bad news,
Yes,
you made my day.

If I
am not
as well
as I thought,
that's
pure gain.

To feel
you're well
is the next best thing
to being well.

I don't feel panic.
I don't feel frantic.
Thank God, my heart
is still joyfully antic.

Something beautiful
has happened to time.
I don't feel
it's running
out on me.
I feel I have
all the time
there is.
Time doesn't belong to me.
I belong to time.

No one is unfortunate
who dies on the upbeat
of life
surrounded by love.

Don't grieve for me.
Grieve for all
who have died,
and will die,
feeling
alone,
abandoned,
unloved.
Weep for them—
Not for me.